piano • vocal • guitar

best of
Depeche Mode

Cover photo © Russell Young/Retna

ISBN 13: 978-1-4234-2181-8
ISBN 10: 1-4234-2181-7

HAL•LEONARD®
CORPORATION
7777 W. BLUEMOUND RD. P.O. BOX 13819 MILWAUKEE, WI 53213

Visit Hal Leonard Online at
www.halleonard.com

BARREL OF A GUN

Words and Music by
MARTIN GORE

DREAM ON

Words and Music by
MARTIN GORE

Medium Electronic Groove

Can you feel _____ a lit - tle love?

As your bon -

Recorded a half step lower.

Dream ____ on, _____ dream ____ on. _____

Dream __

ENJOY THE SILENCE

Words and Music by
MARTIN GORE

All I ev-er want-ed, all I ev-er need-ed __ is here in my __

I FEEL YOU

Words and Music by
MARTIN GORE

*Add upper L.H. notes on 2nd verse only.

PERSONAL JESUS

Words and Music by
MARTIN GORE

(omit R.H. 1st time)

(percussion)

D.S. al Coda

CODA

Reach out, ___ and touch faith.
Your own ___ per -

- son - al Je - sus. ___

34

Reach out, — and touch faith.

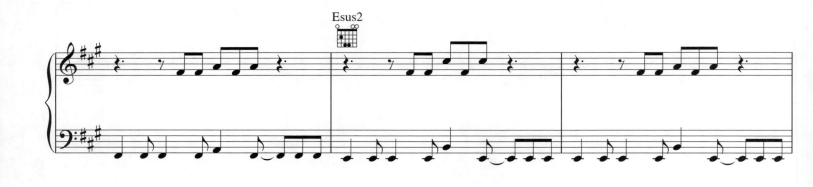

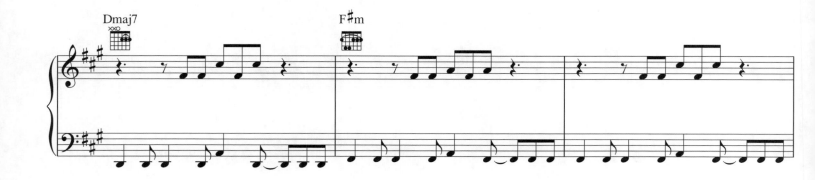

Reach out, ___ and touch faith.

Reach out, __ and touch faith.

IT'S NO GOOD

Words and Music by
MARTIN GORE

Moderately

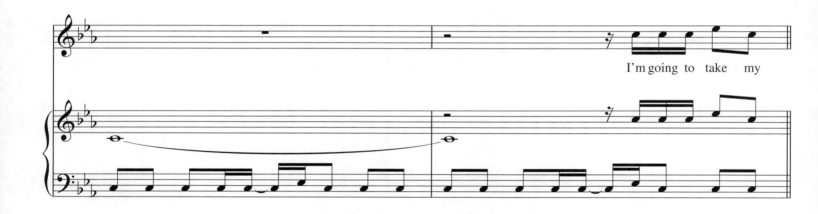

I'm going to take my

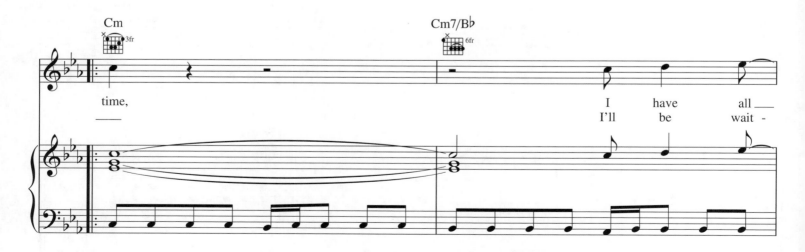

time, ___

I have ___ all ___
I'll be ___ wait-

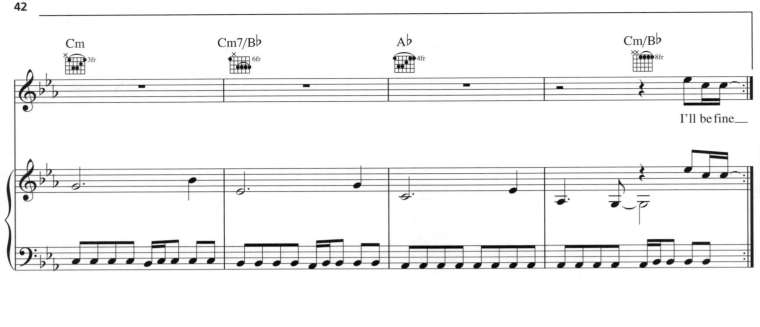

I'll be fine___

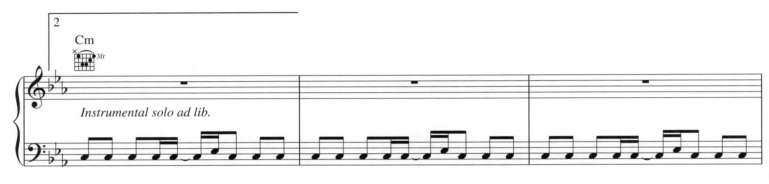

Instrumental solo ad lib.

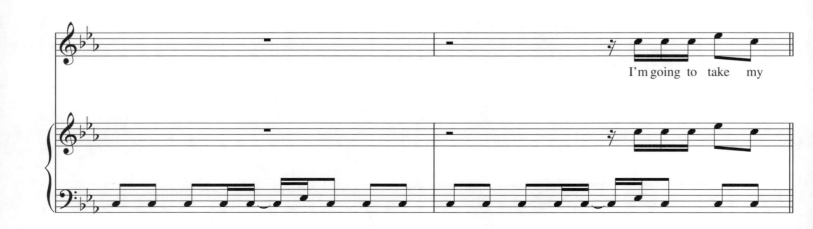

I'm going to take my

me, I know you can't ___ be 'cause

1
it's no good. ___ Don't say you want ___ it's no

2
good. ___

Cm7

Repeat and Fade

JUST CAN'T GET ENOUGH

Words and Music by
VINCE CLARK

When I'm with you, ba - by, I go out _ of my head, and I just can't get e - nough, and I
We walk to - geth - er, we're walk - ing _ down _ the street, and I just can't get e - nough, and I
And when it rains, _ you're shin - ing _ down _ for me, and I just can't get e - nough,

ONLY WHEN I LOSE MYSELF

Words and Music by
MARTIN GORE

*Recorded a half step lower.

PEOPLE ARE PEOPLE

Words and Music by
MARTIN GORE

Bright Industrial Pop

People are people, so why should it be ___ you and I ___ should get a-long so aw-ful-ly? ___

D. S. al Coda

Now you're

CODA

I can't un-der - stand

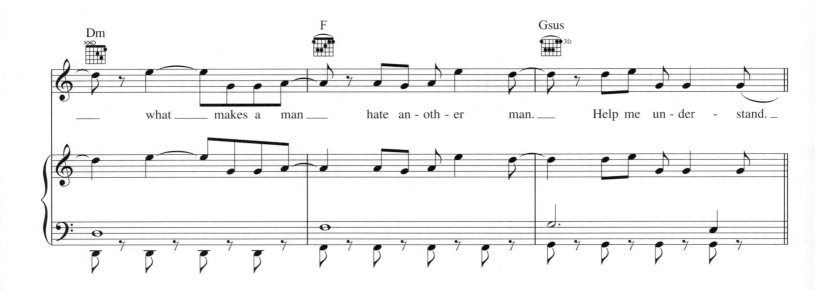

what makes a man hate an - oth - er man. Help me un - der - stand.

POLICY OF TRUTH

Words and Music by
MARTIN GORE

70

PRECIOUS

Words and Music by
MARTIN GORE

*Recorded a half step lower.

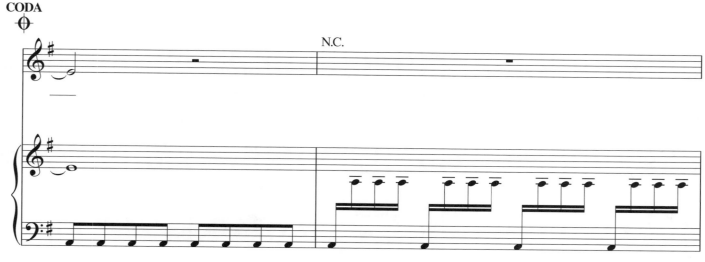

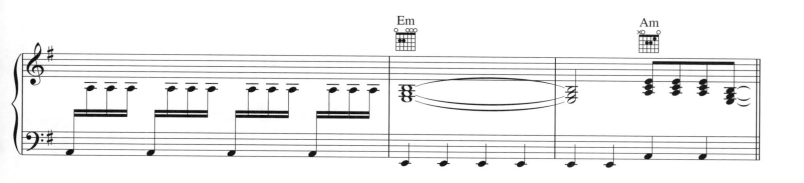

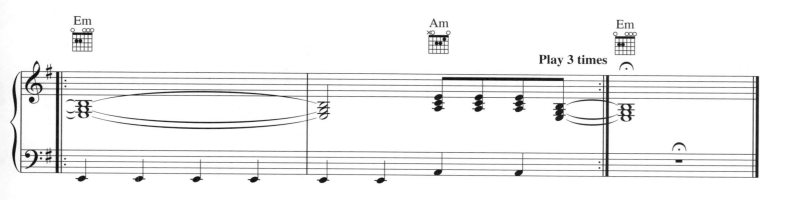

STRANGE LOVE

Words and Music by
MARTIN GORE

WALKING IN MY SHOES

Words and Music by
MARTIN GORE

Laid-back Electronic Groove

I would